Finding Your Stars

Written by Carolyn Morris
Illustrated by Lena Lee

Finding Your Stars
by Carolyn Morris

Copyright ©2022 Carolyn Morris

All rights reserved. No portion of this book may be reproduced in any form without permission from the author, except as permitted by copyright law. For permission, contact: hello@findingyourstars.com

Illustrations by Lena Lee
Proofreading by Jennifer D. Foster, Planet Word

ISBN: 978-1-7778356-0-6

Book design by r/grainger studio, Toronto
Typeset in Sneak by TIGHTYPE™

To Oliver, Reed, Izcalli, Owen, Sebastian and Blake. May you be gentle with your clouds and generous with your stars.
Carolyn Morris

To my loves Riley Kai and Dean. You showed me that through it all (even in the dark), what I need most is to shine my light on the world.
Lena Lee

We each have stars
inside that glow.
They're special skills
and games we know.

Like swinging on
the monkey bars,
dancing, painting,
running far.

At times your stars
are shining bright.
They feel so strong
and real and right.

But then you fall,
and life feels cold.
As clouds move in,
a storm takes hold.

Your clouds are worries,
flaws and fears.
They cover your stars
in gloom and tears.

But there's a curious trick to know

about your clouds
and stars that glow.

Whichever one
you focus on

will build and grow —
so big, so strong.

So if you try to
chase your clouds,
to tell them that
they're not allowed ...

They'll roar with
thunder, rage and rain,
spreading their fears,
their faults, their pain.

But if you greet the
storm, then spin,
back to your stars —
your light within —

You'll start to
rise up to the sky.
Your stars will lift you,
oh so high.

You'll climb right past
the clouds that fade.
They've lost their force —
you're not afraid.

Above you'll see a
wondrous sight.
More lights are
sparkling in the night.

As stars of friends
come into view,
you'll join these
constellations too.

So don't forget how
bright you are.
Embrace your clouds,
then shine those stars.

Carolyn Morris
(The Writer)

Carolyn used to chase her clouds, wishing she could catch sight of stars in the distance. Slowly, she realized her stars and clouds have been within her all along.

These days, Carolyn is a little gentler with her clouds and more generous with her stars. She lives in Toronto with her husband and their two children and loves seeing people shine their stars.

Lena Lee
(The Illustrator)

As a little girl, Lena would get lost in children's books and their illustrations. She would pore over the stories by the dim light of her desk lamp and copy drawings from those books. She learned to draw all kinds of things that way.

As a grown-up, not much has changed. She still loves art, design and storytelling. Lena hopes she can inspire children to embrace their stars and shine brightly, so the world can appreciate their unique talents.

Photos by Dean Vargas

Draw or write some of your **stars**
(things you love to do, things you're good at)
and your **clouds** (things that scare or worry you).

findingyourstars.com

Join us online at findingyourstars.com for more Star and Cloud adventures.

Secret bonuses!
Access additional resources, including printable colouring pages, an audio recording of the book and more, at findingyourstars.com/bonuses

Use the code "STARS"
(Shhh! It's a secret.)

CPSIA information can be obtained
at www.ICGtesting.com
Printed in the USA
LVHW081518300423
745680LV00002B/43